MINIMALISM

How to Simplify Your Life for Stress Relief

(The Practical Guide to Declutter Your Life and Replace the Mindless Stuff)

Stacey Emmons

Published By Zoe Lawson

Stacey Emmons

All Rights Reserved

Minimalism: How to Simplify Your Life for Stress Relief (The Practical Guide to Declutter Your Life and Replace the Mindless Stuff)

ISBN 978-1-77485-312-2

All rights reserved. No part of this guide may be reproduced in any form without permission in writing from the publisher except in the case of brief quotations embodied in critical articles or reviews.

Legal & Disclaimer

The information contained in this book is not designed to replace or take the place of any form of medicine or professional medical advice. The information in this book has been provided for educational and entertainment purposes only.

The information contained in this book has been compiled from sources deemed reliable, and it is accurate to the best of the Author's knowledge; however, the Author cannot guarantee its accuracy and validity and cannot be held liable for any errors or omissions. Changes are periodically made to this book. You must consult your doctor or get professional medical advice before using any of the suggested remedies, techniques, or information in this book.

Upon using the information contained in this book, you agree to hold harmless the Author from and against any damages, costs, and expenses, including any legal fees potentially resulting from the application of any of the information provided by this guide. This disclaimer applies to any damages or injury caused by the use and application, whether directly or indirectly, of any advice or information presented, whether for breach of contract, tort, negligence, personal injury, criminal intent, or under any other cause of action.

You agree to accept all risks of using the information presented inside this book. You need to consult a professional medical practitioner in order to ensure you are both able and healthy enough to participate in this program.

TABLE OF CONTENTS

INTRODUCTION 1

CHAPTER 1: THE HISTORY OF MINIMALISM 4

CHAPTER 2: BENEFITS OF A MINIMALIST LIFE 29

CHAPTER 3: THE IMPORTANCE OF DECLUTTERING 37

CHAPTER 4: STRATEGIES TO STOP PROCRASTINATION 56

CHAPTER 5: WHY WE WANT THINGS WE DON'T NEED? .. 63

CHAPTER 6: MINIMALIZING YOUR SHOPPING 70

CHAPTER 7: HOME 76

CHAPTER 8: ALLOWING YOU TIME TO BREATHE 82

CHAPTER 9: RID OF RELATIONSHIPS THAT ARE TOXIC AND NURTURING THE MOST MEANINGFUL ONES USING MINIMAL 87

CHAPTER 10: PRINCIPLES OF MINIMALISM 94

CHAPTER 11: UNDERSTANDING THE NEED FOR HOARDING 107

CHAPTER 12: WHAT'S THE BEST PLACE DO I BEGIN? 113

CHAPTER 13: CLEANING OUT CLOSETS 121

CHAPTER 14: THE KEYS TO A MINIMALIST LIFESTYLE 141

CHAPTER 15: MINIMALIZING YOUR HOME 148

CHAPTER 16: THE ADVANTAGES OF MINIMALISM + HOW TO IMPLEMENT 154

CHAPTER 17: CLEANING YOUR SPACE **163**

CONCLUSION **182**

Introduction

Minimalism is a concept that is loved by some, but it is also a source of fear for many. There are two extremes of emotions this concept inspires. The most important reason is the widespread misinformation and misconception regarding the concept of minimalism.

Minimalism is a philosophy of easy living. It is among the most popular ideas that will assist you live a life free of stress, obligations and unneeded restrictions. It removes the obstacles that burden you and allows you to have the opportunity to look at life from different perspectives.

If you've been overwhelmed by financial stress and haven't found an escape the shackles, minimalism can aid you in your efforts to reach more financial stability.

If you are feeling that your earnings aren't enough and you are unable to figure out a way to balance your income and expenditures, minimalistism is the best option for you.

It's one of the most effective ways to assist you manage your finances.

Minimalism can also be a good method to create more peace to your life. It assists in making your home more efficient and manageable. It is easier to not be overwhelmed by the sheer volume of your house and the failure to organize and manage the clutter.

This interesting concept assists you to understand the distinction between needs and desires. The majority of our problems today result from our inability to draw an understanding of the difference between these two.

This book will assist you understand the idea of minimalism. It will guide you through the process of implementing minimalist living in your family and the benefits.

It is a comprehensive guide to understanding the crucial strategies to achieve success as well as a warning against the issues.

The book addresses some of the major issues individuals face when they adopt a minimalist lifestyle as a family , and one of them includes children into the program. It's a challenge to integrate children into the process and more difficult to get for them to take their belongings off particularly their toys. This book will provide you with specific plans for introducing children to the process as well as methods you can increase involvement from the kids.

Chapter 1: The History Of Minimalism

The art of minimalism has its own story. This is due to the fact that the yearly gathering of junk didn't begin until the 1920s. There were always people who had useless trinkets and junk however, they were wealthy prior to they experienced the Great Depression. Today, there's the desire to rid ourselves of the stuff we've been over the years, due to the fact that houses are shrinking, even although prices are climbing. Apartments are worth more than homes twenty years ago. Therefore, in order to have enough money to afford a place to live you must reduce your size which means getting rid of things. In medieval times, people never ever disposed of any thing. Even cardboard containers for packing were used to store other items. The things we discard are stored for various uses. Flour bags were used to sew clothes, and leftovers were used to prepare the next food. If you find buttons on the ground and you want to save it as you don't will know when it could come in handy. This idea spread throughout the entire world, and the pandemic spread by generations. Fear of being unclean resulted in people having to hold onto everything. Human beings were compelled to be afraid of turning objects into trash rather than keeping them longer than they were required to. Humans did not ever have to think about minimalism as a matter of fact. In the eighties, minimalism was a reality following the boom of the sixties' economy saw people purchasing all they could. The eighties saw an entire shift.

Materialism became the most human beings in the eighties when it took hold.

Minimalism was a popular trend. Madonna even wrote an anthem about it. Material Girl was a song about being a material girl in a world of fabric and opened up some of the world's minds to the reality that they were focused on the things they have that they were unable to be content with the lifestyle they'd lived. Minimalism stuck on people, super-fast.

The nineties however, witnessed the demise of the initial minimalism wave. The technological revolution made human beings materially loopy again. The new technology was to be purchased otherwise, you'll be judged an outcast. This was translated into other things and the desire to purchase high-end fixtures that be used with the top television and required lots of things that thought of as being rich.

Minimalists did not make an appearance in society until the year the year 2010. Of course, all the time , there were those who had lived their lives with the help of a minimalist living, but it was a situation that often was due to the fact that they had no option.

However, in the year 2018 one millionaire sat on the wind of minimalism and chose to donate one-quarter of his earnings to charities. He discovered that he became more content in this way. Nowadays, a lot of people aren't able to move as far, but it has given those who live there the belief that they must change their lives. They were required to quit living in their belongings and start simply living a life. Today, minimalism is an increasingly well-known concept to a large portion of people. But, it's not a common thing, since the majority of people prefer their smartphones and more relaxed lifestyles.

There are some humans who have lived a minimalist life for a long time. The Amish of the Swiss-Germans believed that if something has to be purchased, you don't require it. They only buy the things they require and only that. Even though certain Amish have adapted and were given mobile phones and motors in emergencies, they still maintain a simple life.

What is MINIMALISM?

A lot of people are awed at what minimalism actually is. You might have also seen the word, but you might not know what it refers to. This is a normal thing. It's not something often discussed in everyday life. This is due to the fact that most people are so absorbed in the materialism of daily life that the thought of cutting certain aspects of life is horrifying. It's not always in the realm of thought of many people nowadays. But, it's slowly becoming more popular in the context of the "Going Green" revolution. It's not always something that is for everyone, but it's something worth thinking about. It is essential to be aware of the things you're thinking about prior to making a choice on what. The book will let you know what you need to know so that you can make a an informed decision on whether you'd like to try this kind of lifestyle or not. If you've decided to be minimalist it is impossible to go back. You'll have to share your way of living with everyone else which is the meaning of it's a way of life. You must be organized to discover alternatives that are different from others that surround you, and who may be able to consider you to be as a nutcase. A few people are able to comprehend the idea that you could be content without having a lot of stuff. The concept of minimalism is cutting down the requirement of "stuffs" within your home to the minimum of essentials. It's all about removing all excess from your life and focusing on the things you need to live your life. A lot of people struggle with this concept because they feel that because they worked for so long to acquire what they possess, that they shouldn't have to do it so as they feel satisfied. It is true that you should let go of everything to feel satisfied. However when you don't sacrifice the pleasures then you can't claim that you live the minimalist life because this is the definition of minimalism: living with the smallest quantity of possessions you are able to.

Minimalism is about finding pleasure in being alive. It's about opening your eyes and observing your surroundings better than you've ever seen before. It's time to get your life back and not letting your possessions of cloth over you. There is a lot of minimalism, and then there is a simple minimalistism. In the process of deliberating about minimalism, a lot of people immediately jump into the extremes. But, there are a few of us who are enough to reach that point. There are many levels of minimalistism. Many people just give up items that they do not need, and certain people reside in tiny shacks eating berries and bark which they find in nature. It's based on your level of comfort, not your own comfort level. However, there are a few benefits to choosing this lifestyle. The blessings listed below.

Who IS PERSONALIZED As A MINIMALIST?

A minimalist is free of the unneeded items of daily life in order to create space for the things which makes you feel happy. It's a way to eliminate clutter in all forms leaving the space for peace, freedom and the feeling of lightness. A minimalist is one who rejects the notion of excess, of getting and eating and shopping for greater size is more beneficial. A minimalist instead is one who believes in the benefits of being less, a life of contentment in what we value and the things that make us truly happy. A minimalist recognizes that having more things doesn't bring us happiness. Earning more money and being more are of no use. The idea of filling your life with stress and affluence is not ideal and an undesirable thing to avoid. A minimalist is one who values the quality of life, not the quantity, in all its forms. Being a minimalist is incredibly satisfying. It is possible to wake up in an hour in a space free of clutter, within the peace of early morning, sip coffee, read, go to run and later write. Do a bit more work and spend time with my personal family. These are the things that bring you joy. You're not buying a variety of items. Not travelling all the time, and not going to events , or investing in expensive entertainment. I don't watch television, and am not constantly bombarded by advertisements. Some people might find pleasure in these experiences but I'm not condemning them. I'm merely stating what I would like to be content from my simple experience. It's the most important thing. Determine your passions and what makes you happy. Remove all the other stuff, so you can make room for the important things. It's not living a life of nothing, or boredom. It's an existence of wealth with less. Your minimalist life might be more specific as mine. You'll have to figure out the things that make you happy. Plan your ideal day. Remove yourself from unnecessary things, in order to create space for this exceptional day for the people and things you cherish. This book should guide you to that direction. The concept of minimalism not have to be limited to involve cleaning, decluttering garage bins, or redecorating the walls of your home however, you could be in the wrong. Let me try and provide an explanation for this lifestyles-converting exercise. Minimalism is a way of bringing awareness to and controlling the people and gadgets that we allow to enter our lives. That's right, human beings. Humans and devices need time and energy from us, and these are items we would not wish to throw away. Pay attention to experiences instead of possessions. The ability to create wonderful memories of good friends and family is often a lot more than the stuff that are currently stuffed into the cabinets and other storage spaces. The notion of all people starting out as minimalists is a fascinating one.

when you look back There isn't an person who came into the world with things that were in their possession. Every person started as minimalists. The value of our lives isn't what we can measure by our possessions. Possessions may make us happy good for a short time. Material possessions that aren't needed eat up our time, power, and our freedom. I believe that minimalists are beginning to realize the fact that. It is easy to agree by the energizing feeling of de-cluttering as well as cutting down even though there are a lot of things to you can't get rid of at home right this moment. This is due to the fact that we've all experienced an similar situation at some point or another. For instance, think of going on an excursion. When you leave you're likely trying to pack your bags at the last moment. You go through the list of things you need to carry with you, and despite the fact that everything is in order but you're left with the feeling you've left out. However, the time is ticking, and you're about to leave. You get up, stand up, shut the door within the back of you, and start walking your suitcase down the road with an eerie sensation of freedom. You believe that, yes you can be there for a few minutes using this suitcase. Perhaps you've neglected to pack something. but you'll be able to find something you require wherever you go. When you arrive at your holiday place and settle on your freshly-made mattress. It's a good feeling. The space is clean and clear. There isn't any of the things that normally take your attention, the things that take up a lot of your time. This is why hotels often are so relaxing. You feel a little numb to your feet, as if you could continue to walk for hours. You are free to go wherever you'd like. Your time is at your disposal and you're not weighed down by the same routine jobs or chores that weigh on your shoulders. This is a minimal state and all humans have had professional life at some point or another. It's not the same, also, however. Imagine your go back flight. Even though your belongings have been well-packed into your luggage before the time you began your journey but the entire thing has been squeezed into an unorganized mess. The things you bought aren't fit in the suitcase, and you're also carrying several enormous paper bags. Tickets to admission and receipts from the tourism websites you've visited, which will be entered into these later, aren't they? This is why they're even stuffed with pockets. You're inside the security line and the moment is now to get your tickets to board. You're wondering where you found it? You look everywhere, but you are unable to find it. You're heading towards toward the highest point of the road and your frustration increases. You feel the cold gazes of other people who may be in the extended line within the lower back of your are concerned that your back is being cut by means of needles and pins. It's a condition of maximalists. The most stressful times are likely to occur when you're juggling more things than you're able to manage. It's difficult to separate what's essential. As we strive to get more, we find ourselves having to spend more time and energy to hold and control everything we have. We are so determined to accomplish this to the point that things that have been designed to aid us become our own.

How MINIMALISM Changes your life

Now we're back at the original question. What is the reason for minimalism? The fact is, the reason is different for each person. What works for you may not work for someone else and what is effective for someone else may be a different story for you. Yet, every person is able to benefit from this way of life. No matter if you go through the big way or small distances the benefits are numerous. advantages that there will be something for anyone. Even if it's just keeping some things out of the way and getting rid of your pile of items before turning into hoarder. Don't be silly; it's an issue for some. Particularly as they reach the age of dementia. The less stuff you own at the beginning the harder it is for you to become hoarder. You must ensure that you keep your level of clutter before you go over.

Minimalism could bring an opportunity to bring back your life in the manner described in the previous paragraph. If you feel as if that you're weighted down by chains and balls You will discover that you're not content, and you'll be feeling that your life isn't yours to live. You must strive to restore your life in order to achieve some sort of satisfaction again. A minimalist lifestyle will help you be yourself and to not be a slave to anyone other than yourself because you'll be at odds to none. You might have a couple of possessions, but your neighbor could have everything that he needs, and putting his life to purchase the fancy items he owns, and in the meantime you're earning savings because you're saving money and you're not buying all those extravagant gadgets.

There's a lot of joy knowing that if the latest mobile phone comes out, you will not have to buy it. Because , in the past, whenever the latest Smartphone is released the older model is sold at a fraction of the price.

If you reside in the Midwest this could mean one month's rent in a beautiful house and the cost of electric and fuel. If you're satisfied with your possessions then you don't have to be concerned about what other have since you, absolutely will not be concerned. When you're not concerned, they might feel like their possessions were not worth a thing, and is exactly what it is. The reason you buy expensive devices is to impress people. What else is the reason to throw away a TV that is purposefully designed in order to purchase one that does the same thing , but is larger? If you are feeling that you shouldn't be able to impress everyone, all material objects will seem stale. This is what minimalism is. Understanding that you're in a race without any other than yourself and that objects of material don't aid you in achieving your goals.

Quick! I want to know the most joyful and some may even call it the most jolly person in history, whether historical or contemporary history.

Okay, except for Doris Day. The person I'm referring to, as it is revealed, doesn't exist, and this could be the reason why she seems to be so blissfully always happy.

This is about the singular Santa Claus. Father Christmas. Pere Noel. He is renowned all over the world for "making an inventory and then reviewing the list twice."

When you think about it, the good ole Santa is a stressful person to be around that is so stressful in fact that it's a good thing he's only required to perform it once per year. Even though he is clearly advanced in age and not in top physical shape He is still tasked with the enormous responsibility of providing gifts for the holidays to all the children of the world. In fact, to all the children who are good at all.

Given the high anxiety that will be part and parcel of this massive job, he's always calm, focused and at ease. Could this be due to him making lists and checks them at least twice?

My opinion is that creating lists is an easy and extremely beneficial method to fight anxiety, stress and depression, restoring your tranquility as well as maintaining your optimistic and positive outlook.

In this article, I will provide some essential list of techniques which will allow and help you to live a healthier and more efficient life.

Your List of Your Favorite Things

The first list might be referred to as "These are some of my top things."

The classic song in The Sound of Music is not one of your top things, and could frustrate you to the point of insanity considering your current state of mind, then take my apologies. However, the truth is the idea behind this song, which revolves around finding the bleakness of a day by recommending some guaranteed positive things to do--is a highly suggested one.

Try it out. However you feel, how stressed, or depressed your life seems at any time take a moment to think about the things that are guaranteed to make you smile. things in life, large or small and minor, that bring satisfaction to you.

A beautiful day. A romantic evening with your loved one. A favorite movie or song. A passion or sport you love. Food you enjoy. A book that you enjoy reading over and over. It's a fun thing to do and enjoy with your family and family and friends.

If you ever feel depressed or stressed take a look at the Favorite Things list and reflect about the blessings that fill and enrich your life. You may not be aware of the amount of things to cherish and love.

As I was creating my own individual list, began to think about the small things that give me a flash of happiness every single day. The butterfly's flight and the gorgeous butterfly flies free in my backyard. The joy of my best friend, whose love and encouragement through the toughest of moments has been a blessing to me. The tune of a beloved track whenever it is played at the radio station, which makes me smile each time I listen to it. The aroma that comes from my mother's delicious chocolate chip cookie recipes exquisite and delicious. The sensation of pure joy that I experience when I watch an inspiring, top-quality film like Field of Dreams, Singin In the Rain, or Casablanca. I soon realized that the old saying is real: small things matter lots, and the smallest things could be truly amazing!

If possible try taking a few minutes to relax and enjoy an activity that is on your agenda. You can read a few pages from your favorite book, and then escape to the fantastical, fictional world it provides for your enjoyment. Take a bite of hot fudge sundaes or a slice of apple pie should they be as one of your top desserts. Begin by meeting your spouse or a close friend for a short lunch, and talk about the highlights that you've had in your life. Join a team, or a club, whether locally or online which will enable you to pursue your preferred pastime or interest. Enjoy that music you love before you head to work, preparing your body for a fresh and better day.

As for that new and improved day, my second list could better be described as a schedule for the day.

Make a List of Your Day

It is likely that you already have the list each day in one form or another. Keep an agenda or a day-timer that lists your scheduled activities, both professional and personal for the day. What I'm soliciting you to do however is to include a couple of fun and enjoyable activities in the midst of the meetings and shifts. This way, you will be able to ensure that you dedicate a portion of the day to a satisfying and energizing experience that you can anticipate on your busiest days or the most difficult days.

When you're done with every day, make sure to write down or draw a hurriedly drawn star to each activity which you have completed successfully. This doesn't need to be anything major If you've remembered to clean up your trash each morning, you can earn yourself an award. If you assist a coworker complete a project on time so that they can meet the deadline for that day, you deserve an award. If you spend time with your dog during the evening, treat him/her to an indulgence and avoid shouting whenever they drop an unattractive calling card on the carpet...well you'll know what I mean.

You might be amazed by how rich and fulfilled your life has become and along with that knowledge will come a sense happiness and satisfaction that is sure to provide you with a sense of joy that is unexpected.

Chapter 2: Benefits of A Minimalist Life

Have you ever noticed that people of today are prone to reciting negative mantras?

The majority of complaints disguise as excuses for failing to accomplish what the want or need to do.

The positive side is that for the majority of these frequently repeated words, minimalism can be a solution or at a minimum, some relief.

Minimalism can assist you in avoiding making these famous statements:

"I don't have time!"

It is true that your free moment is proportional to the amount of chores. The more chores you have to do, the more free time to spend time with other activities, such as familytime, visiting or reading, or watching a great movie. The tasks that take up your time can be made easier by reducing, removing or even deleting off your calendar.

"I'm always in debt!"

As with the relation between tasks and time The value of your bank account is proportional to the quantity of items you invest in frequently unknowingly, buying impulse items.

"I have too many things to clean/organize!"

The principle is straightforward The more stuff there are in your workplace or at home, the more work you'll need to tidy and organize. How long do you have to spend cleaning all the small items from your cabinets? Do all of these items really be needed?

If you consider what you actually own it might be easier to put aside the things you don't own. The concept of minimalism makes evident that if you do not have no need for something material such as an outfit that you like, you don't need to. Because that you're here, I'm certain you're richer than the majority of people around the globe. Even if you have to sacrifice certain things, still have plenty.

However, remember that the concept of minimalism is not a miracle. It isn't possible to change your life overnight just because you've got less things. It's an ongoing process, but it's a method that aids people and helps people change their lives for the better.

The true price of everything

We frequently think about reducing the number of purchases we do every day, mostly due to the thought of our finances, particularly in times of economic turmoil. What we seldom ever think about is the worth of the items we purchase does not only depend on the cost.

The cost of purchasing an item is only the beginning of the of the iceberg. When we purchase an item that we want to keep, we put it in our homes, to our lives, and are adding one more thing to the world.

This object was not created on a shelf in a shop it was a product of forests (if comprised of wood) or mines (if constructed from iron) and from the deepest parts of the earth (if made of plastic and other synthetic substances that are derived from petroleum) or perhaps the combination of all three possibilities. The object came from the natural resources, and therefore it was created in a manufacturing facility - which is a source of pollution. It is then developed and distributed to different distribution centers before finally going to the retailer. However, this isn't the final stage.

The existence of this object has only begun to be a part of our lives, even though we've been paying for all the damage it has caused in order to be able to possess it.

Once you have purchased it, you will need to get it home via car, making another route that pollutes, using a delivery service, which , in addition to causing pollution, also costs money.

After all the expenses in terms of time, money, and resources, the object now takes the space of our offices or homes and offices, which can be used for different reasons or might not even have to be there at all. With fewer objects, it's possible to reside in smaller spaces, which could save you money, lots of money. But this is just one step in the cycle of objects. If it's electronic, it needs power (or even more important batteries) such as. It also requires regular maintenance and cleaning as well as or configuration. This demands both physical and time.

When you buy new items take note of the path it took to reach your hands.

The carbon footprint

Apart from the obvious benefits that we have more cash in our accounts, more room and less cost to the earth, using less and living a more simple life can reduce our carbon footprint.

A carbon footprint can be described as the kind of environmental footprint we leave on the planet - directly linked to the loop an item makes around the world before it reaches your home, as we have just considered.

It assesses the amount of carbon dioxide that we generate, either in a direct or indirect way and the ways in which this emission of gases affects the environmental conditions. Carbon dioxide is produced every day, as we go about our day-to-day routines, and this carbon dioxide is released in the air. It is the primary cause of the greenhouse effect as well as global warming.

Carbon dioxide - also known as footprint size - created by every person is different, dependent on their individual life style. Research has shown that on average, each person produces 4 tons of gas each year, but that varies greatly between countries - for instance in the US the average person generates upwards of 20 tons of carbon dioxide each year!

If you'd like to take a into consideration the amount of carbon dioxide you emit You are welcome to go to:

https://www.carbonfootprint.com/calculator.aspx

The lower carbon footprint of every person can be added to the list of benefits that we can reap from minimalism.

Certain products because they are so ubiquitous in our everyday life, it is extremely difficult to reduce the carbon footprint since we're always consume without considering the effects. One of the most effective examples is our clothes and fashion that will be the topic of the following chapter.

Chapter 3: The Importance of Decluttering

It is a hassle to sort through clutter. It can increase the time to finish and, most of the time it takes longer to sort rather than actually working. So, mess of any kind isn't good for anyone. But, just talking about the negative consequences on clutter can be one thing but the actual action to address it is a different matter altogether.

We don't realize that we're overwhelmed by mental, physical as well as emotional clutter. It's anything that's not serving any function within your daily life. However, from relationships, memories, and memorabilia our minds, hearts and homes are full of clutter.

This mess not only makes the task of sorting out things difficult, but also puts us in a perpetual battle. It constantly throws the issue of choice in our faces. The power of "choice" might seem like something that is lucrative however, when your brain is constantly forced to make decisions at every turn in the course of your life, it can start becoming unfocused about the choices.

For example, you get up early in the morning to prepare for your office. The first task is to pick from the two dozen clothes in your wardrobe. The process of selecting the appropriate shoes could take about five minutes. It's not the reason of the item that has confused you but the overwhelming quantity of choices. Anything that causes you to take unneeded choices in your life is causing confusion in your brain and your life.

Have you ever had a the thought that the most successful individuals around the globe such as Mark Zuckerberg, Steve Jobs and Barak Obama seem to appear often in similar clothes? Despite earning billions of dollars of revenue the successful do not seem to wear designer clothes or accessories. The reason is quite easy, they've grasped the importance of being capable of making sound crucial, well-thought out, and conscious choices, they need to be able to stay away from the exhaustion caused by these minor decisions. If your brain is engaged in making such decisions regardless of the situation that it is occupied, your mind will be exhausted.

The most interesting aspects is that the majority of people do not know about this mess. They might be spending an hour each day searching for keys. The search for the right outfit could take up more than 10 minutes every day. It is possible that they are wasting hours each day with someone they dislike. They do not recognize that the things they have are just clutter. They aren't the things that deserve some place in their lives.

We continue to ignore these issues for too long, only to eventually make them a element of our daily lives. This is followed by sobbing and cribbing. We're discontent, depressed and confused. We could have avoided all this by identifying the clutter and eliminated it. Clearing out clutter not only gives you time but can also help you save lots of money, mental pain suffering, pain, and anguish.

To live a happy prosperous, successful, and prosperous life, it's vital to eliminate the clutter from your life. This chapter will assist you identify the clutter and figuring out how to clear it out.

Physical Clutter

Physical clutter is anything in your vicinity but is not that you can use immediately. It could have served a purpose at some point in time and may prove useful in the future, however, If it's not being used right now then it shouldn't be around. It's creating chaos. It can make your work more difficult and long for you. It is best to eliminate it.

If you own 10 tops and have worn four since they're your tops The remaining six are creating clutter. They're taking up space in your wardrobe. They demand a bit of your time every day. Sometimes they might cause you to think about the point of purchasing them. Even though they are unlikely to be worn, they'll need to be cleaned and stored. Similar is the case for the additional pair of pants, shoes and other items.

This is also true for the kitchen. There are likely to be many pans and pots that have been not being utilized. Silverware that hasn't been cleaned out for months. There are appliances aren't used or have better alternatives to them. We'll never be rid of old appliances. We entertain ourselves with the thought that they'll one day prove useful. However, they'll cause the clutter each day that they're not being utilized.

The living rooms of our homes are filled with things that aren't meant to live in. They are simply overflowing with clutter. This causes us to work every day to clean and organize things. The more thingsto be organized, the more amount of time needed to keep them well-organized.

Minimalism is the act of identifying items that you truly use and want and eliminating the remainder. It aids to identify the items you don't need or need. It encourages you to get rid of them to make room for fewer items to clean and organize. So, you can be able to spend more time with yourself and your family. De-cluttering you home and your belongings is the initial step to minimalism.

Mental Clutter

We don't realize that mental clutter is equally significant issue within our daily lives, just like physical clutter. Mental clutter has dominated our lives to the degree that we've lost the ability to live our lives consciously. The mind is always occupied to something. When you first get up in the morning, your brain is busy. If you're cleaning the teeth, or getting dressed the morning routine, your brain is engaged in one thing or another and telling you to move on with your the day.

The only thing lacking from the entire procedure is the will. There's no intention for it, just following instructions. These directions are merely a continuation of the events from the previous day commitments, obligations, commitments and so on.

We've abandoned having a life as free and intelligent human beings. We are always busy making decisions, but the majority of the decisions in our lives are taken by those who we feel obligated to.

There is always pressure to keep jobs. The excitement of doing an assignment flawlessly isn't so much as the fear of losing the job. When someone is hired where the pay is not high and the work experience is not as good however, the motivation to do the job is extremely high. In time, that enthusiasm fades because of stress of earning more money and keeping the lifestyle. Then, you stop working to improve your skills and begin working toward saving your job.

We are prone to being in the company of those we dislike for the simple reason that it is crucial, which causes our minds to be overwhelmed with chaos. We always face the issue of the issue of decision fatigue. We are constantly mumbling words. We are constantly planning and plotting in our heads as we're constantly trapped between the devil and the vast blue sea.

It's not without consequence. Body and mind have to work together. Stress and mental fatigue take their physical toll on overall health. It has a significant influence on our behaviour. We tend to avoid those we shouldn't and could. Our relationships start getting strained. Our family lives get affected. Stress can cause anxiety and suffering, and people seek comfort in shopping. We attempt to fix the situation by giving things to people to whom we should have paid attention to, time and love.

The process of decluttering the mind is an essential aspect of being a minimalist. It aids in organizing your thoughts and getting your priorities in order. Most of the time both of you have the same needs but it can be difficult to stay on the same line. This isn't the result of a lack of coordination, or chemical imbalance. It's about an insufficient space since there is too much chaos everywhere.

When your thoughts are sorted and your priorities set You'll find it effortless to connect with family members and comprehend their needs.

It is time to let go of the chains that hold you and discover your true self. You'll need to conduct an honest self-analysis and determine the most important aspects you desire from your life. You must realize that there is no point in having things that don't add any value and begin eliminating them in the shortest time possible. The process of decluttering your mind can assist your family members as well as you to become a more minimalist family.

Decluttering

De-cluttering involves identifying and removing things, thoughts, or people who don't add any worth to your life. Everything you have around you should have value, and this is vitally important.

De-cluttering Your Home

The process of decluttering your house can assist to simplify things for your home front. After you have cleared out your home you'll feel free. Being free of all the items that served nothing but needed maintenance and work provides an incredible feeling. This book will explain the best ways to clean your home with great detail. It will guide you through the steps to clean every part within your residence. But, the most important factor you'll have to keep in mind is take a look at every item within your home to determine its "value proposition". If it is providing anything of worth to your life on a regular basis, it should be kept or, if not, it will need to move on.

Your home should be welcoming but should not turn into an unintentional treasure chest where you have to search for items. Everything should be accessible and have an appropriate place.

It is a good idea to keep your surfaces clean. The floors of your home tables and counter tops and benches, dressers, and any other flat surfaces should be clean of any clutter. You may have some things for decoration purpose, but you should not have anything more than that. Get rid of things that aren't needed. You should only keep artwork or other decorative items that are of real value to you. Do not hang things on your wall just for just the sake of it. Be aware that getting rid of objects is a habit which needs to be taught and it may be challenging initially.

Furniture is essential to live an enjoyable life. But, we rarely think about the amount of furniture actually need. We are quick to purchase things we love, but we seldom exhibit the same amount of enthusiasm about getting rid of things that require replacement by the new furniture. Furniture is moved around to other rooms, or within the same space. It serves no purpose whatsoever and only creates mess and maintenance schedule. Consider the furniture you require and keep only the items that add significant value to your life. Don't store things within your home just because they're not bothering you. Tossing out garbage and other items are a manner of life that has to be broken and is quite difficult at first.

Do the same thing and determine the items you have in your kitchen and bedrooms. Your wardrobes could need a full day of work and present the greatest challenge.

But, decluttering is the most effective method to control your house and your life. The more messy your home is, the more difficult it is for you to maintain control.

De-cluttering Your Mind

The process of clearing the mind is crucial. The constant battle is a part of our lives, and the inability to see the joy surrounding us is the cause of mental chaos. Our minds are overloaded with thoughts at all times that they are unable to see the joy around. You won't be able to feel the flavor of the world's most delicious gourmet meal if you're is focused on the criticism you're likely to receive at work from the boss. You will not feel the beauty of the weather if are always late to work.

It's not the entire world that is unhappy, it's the person within you who has lost motives to be content. The world is as stunning as it was. The rivers are still wild, the oceans are still roaring while the mountains are high, and the skies are still extremely blue. Rain still gets us wet, and the dew drops shine in the morning sun.

As John Keats said:

"A beauty-related thing can be forever a delight:

Its beauty grows; it will never go to the void;"

It's just our inability to appreciate things that are beautiful. We're so enslaved in our minds that we don't see the beauty that is happening around us. We are unable to listen to the quiet demands of our beloved family members. We don't pay attention to the emotions of our loved ones. We ignore the calls of our children. In spite of this, we continue to search for admiration, love and appreciation from outside.

If we don't get our thoughts straightened out in our heads it will be impossible to be able to feel content around. It is crucial to acknowledge the importance of clearing the mind.

The primary reason for mental stress is because individuals have enslaved themselves to responsibilities they do not wish to take on. This causes them to scream every day and force people to feel unsatisfied. Let yourself loose. Let yourself breathe.

Remove yourself from situations that cause you pain and suffering. If your job isn't satisfying find a new one which will assist you to be content. Make time for activities that will bring you joy and happy. If being around several individuals makes you feel uncomfortable, you should stay clear of them. Don't stay in the crowd.

The process of clearing your thoughts and thinking about what you can do to bring happiness is vital. A person who is unhappy will create more discontent around. The sooner you are aware of this the more positive.

How Do I Begin?

Living a simple life as the family can be difficult for some. Inviting all family members to the same table could be difficult since family members may not think alike at first. But, it's not something that isn't attained. This book will assist you understand the ways to instill a minimalist approach into your family members and encourage them to adopt a minimalist life. The book will also provide the steps to follow for the best results.

The most important thing to be aware of is that it is a new path so you could have some issues at first. But, there's no reason to be concerned as it will assist you live an enlightened and peaceful life. Once you are accustomed to your new lifestyle, you'll enjoy a great sense of freedom and pleasure.

You'll need to become sensible and fair to your family members and yourself. Don't rush through the process or make others do it for you. This is something everyone in your family must be able to love and will require some time. Continue to follow the path of minimalism to find peace happiness, harmony, and peace within your own life.

Chapter 4: Strategies to Stop Procrastination

Many people like postponing stressful work in favor engaging in enjoyable activities first. Some people prefer working under stress, and that's why they can justify putting off duties until they feel pressured by the time they have left prior to the deadline.

Procrastination can be the result of a variety of causes, such as pressure, loss of productivity, laziness anxiety, guilt and also lower self-esteem due to reactions to failures from others or not executing the obligations or obligations. Procrastination can be further aggravated when these emotions are felt simultaneously.

It is believed to be commonplace for individuals to put off their work up to a certain extent in particular if their job is difficult or dull. This becomes a problem but when it hinders everyday activities due to grave, yet unsubstantiated motives.

Procrastination is an incredibly destructive behavior and lots of people are attracted by it. These are helpful suggestions in overcoming procrastination so that you can increase your productivity at work and in other pursuits.

Take on your fears. Procrastination can be caused by anxiety. What is the fear? There are a lot of anxieties when you work. The fear of failing can lead you to stop and delay your work. You may be scared to fail, which is the reason you are unable to begin working on your project. In some instances there are people who fear failure. Always be prepared to face and overcome your fears. This is an excellent way to overcome your procrastination inclination.

Create lists. Task lists can be helpful to keep the track of your accomplishments. With lists like this it is easy to get people inspired to finish every task at an agreed time. In the list, add the date for each task and assign it a deadline. This way you'll feel a little stress to complete the task when the deadline is near.

Divide and overcome. If you're given massive tasks, tackling them head-on could lead to you succumbing to anxiety and stress. That's why most people who are given these projects feel overwhelmed or depressed simply by looking at the volume of work involved. In this situation it's better to divide the work into distinct segments and then complete them in one step. It is possible to make an outline of the separated parts of the project and choose which one to begin. So you will be able to work on the biggest project and not be aware of how large it actually is.

Be aware of the behavior and take action. Once you start working on you have on your list, thoughts of putting off work will eventually appear in your mind, particularly in the presence of distractions and temptations all around you. At some point you might think "I'll be able to do this sooner" or "I have plenty of enough time tomorrow, so I'll play until the moment". If these thoughts are forming in your mind, then it is an indication that you're trying to put off the task or delay. It is important to recognize the signs and do to avoid giving the temptation. Instead, begin taking on the task. You will soon realize that the task becomes much easier once you've begun working on it.

The world around you will disappear. If you have distracting factors around you You'll be extremely difficult to complete your work in time. While watching TV can be difficult , particularly in the case that your favorite program is playing, the same applies when you're working on a computer , and your Facebook page is up. While you're doing something remove all distractions and focus solely on the task at hand.

Do yourself a favor and reward yourself to a job that you've done well. When you complete a project, it feels great even if it's part of the task that you completed. When you've completed a portion of your task you can reward yourself by indulgence into activities that you find amusing and enjoyable. You can enjoy your favorite snack, catch up on your favorite television show or play video games. Make sure to limit your reward to just an hour or so and accomplish a different task for two more hours of entertainment. Intoxicated and forgetting to complete your task is also a type of procrastination.

Jam. There are other things that can constitute distractions however music isn't the only one. If you're bored when working on a task, wear earphones and enjoy your preferred track. The music you listen to will put you in the mood to work and motivate you throughout the work.

Meditate. There is a time and a place for every thing. There is time to work, catch up on television and listen to music take a bite, and even sleep. You must also be able to relax and be still for a few minutes. You don't need to do anything. Just be still and breathe. This helps you relax from the stress of your job and reenergizes your spirit. A American young man once asked an Chinese monk "What If I'm unable to carry them, what happens is the likelihood of me dying?" The monk answered: "Don't forget to breathe." Breathing in silence and not thinking about anything is the most simple way to relax, so don't forget to breathe.

Whatever methods you've read, actually implementing them is not the same. Combating procrastination isn't always as simple as reading about the ways to overcome it. The desire to delay important tasks is strong and for many, it is difficult to combat.

Chapter 5: Why We Want Things We Don't Need?

Before we dive in reducing our belongings let's discuss the reasons we are compelled to purchase so many things. What led us to the point we are at now? Our emotions, along with various forces are at work against us since the modern era. Businesses realize that people purchase emotions, not things. For instance, Harley Davidson is not the top motorcycle you can purchase at a reasonable price but when you invest in the Harley you are buying into the mystery, personality and how it can make you feel. Harley owners have an elitist following for the brand. They have all the clothes as well as the tattoos of the logo and are a part of Harley groups. If you're a owner and are upset because I did not say that it's the most reliable motorcycle you could purchase at a reasonable price, then you've an emotional connection to the company.

In the past when people were buying items they required. In the end the Industrial Age brought about mass production of products which were usually hand-crafted. The wages also increased, and Americans began eating more. Fast forward to the 1920's. Sigmund Freud's son, Edward Bernays was an Austrian-American who was referred to as, "The Father of Consumerism". Bernays employed psychoanalysis in order to convince people to purchase items they didn't really require. At first, he was referring to his techniques as "propaganda" however the Nazis took over this term in World War II, and it was he who created"Public Relations. "Public Relations". Bernays also called it "Consent Engineering". The first time he used psychoanalysis was to help consumers when a cigarette manufacturer wanted to attract the female market to take up smoking. In the early days there were only male smokers. Bernays hired beautiful, young females to smoke what called "Torches of Liberty" at the New York Easter Parade in 1929. He then approached the press and explained to them that these women were showing that they were just like men by smoking their torch of freedom. The media took pictures and before long, newspapers across the country carried pictures of these independent, strong gorgeous women smoking. The strategy worked, and the sale of cigarettes to women increased dramatically. Tobacco companies created cigarettes especially for females. Later on, advertising campaigns such as "You've made a great stride baby" were designed.

We are bombarded with advertisements that are created to make us purchase things that we don't really require. We've all been sucked into it, possibly because we didn't realize the emotional impact of buying. There is a saying that you shouldn't force someone to purchase something they don't need However, you can induce them to purchase items they don't really need. Today, we are aware and are aware of how our emotions affects our purchasing choices.

Sugar High

There is a sense of emotion associated with the loss or gain of possessions. We've all purchased something (or in my case, lots of things) and felt the excitement when we left the shop with that unique item that we have to have. It's similar to an adrenaline rush. It is similar to a sugar high then use it just for a few times, and it's not utilized. Sometimes it's left in our home for a long time without being used. The sugar rush doesn't last very long however there is the instant when you feel happy. People always seek pleasureand will go to any lengths to stay away from pain. The idea of the satisfaction of purchasing that product which makes one feel happy is a more attractive thought to some than the thought of going out without the product. Going out of the store without that item might be associated with feelings like "I would like to have it but I can't afford this" as well as "Everyone else has it, so why shouldn't me?"

Look at your home. Are you able to remember buying everything you have? Do you remember when that little thing that corner was cool? Do not feel guilty. Advertisers use our emotions to make us buy products and even promote for these items. Check out all the vehicles in the roadways with logos and labels on their vehicles. Do the driver right in front of you who wears an Yeti cooler sticker and a Costa sunglasses on his vehicle actually care about the brands so significantly? Are we really concerned whether he endorses these items? No. They might be excellent products, but there's an explanation for why people feel strongly about these products. The man believes he's part of a community or something like, "I can afford a $2000 cooler and expensive glasses". There's a reason an individual such as Bill Gates does not have an "Yeti" label on their Bentley. Gates doesn't feel that being part of this particular group. Advertisers have targeted specifically the people in this category and they have an established image associated with their product.

The truth is that there's an emotional component to buying things we don't really require. We think that they will make us feel more comfortable. We experience a brief sensation of being happy and feeling like a part of something greater than ourselves. Sometimes, it's because of jealousy. Sometimes , people are trying to compensate for something that is missing from our lives. The most important thing is to realize that there is an emotional component when we purchase things that we don't really need. Being aware of the emotional aspect we buy can help us stop and contemplate the next purchase. Knowing the emotional connection to our possessions will help us reduce their size and keep us from getting into the same position time and time.

Chapter 6: Minimalizing Your Shopping

When you shop you'll notice that you leave with items you've had no intention of buying. You might think that it's smart to buy possible Christmas gifts in June, but it's not really that smart at all. At the time Christmas rolls around, your priorities will be different the same way they have for others. If you're looking to put aside money for Christmas, you can begin with your savings for shopping and put them into a savings account at the bank, so that by Christmas, you'll have plenty of money to travel out and purchase presents. Take a look at the next batch of items in your trolley , and then lay everything you purchased on the table. Sort it into different piles. You will be amazed by the details of your buying habits.

Fourth Step: Clean the grocery list

The piles must be labeled:

Essentials

Non healthy snacks

Foods that are healthy

Non-essential extras

Nobody is saying that you should purchase things at a bargain price. If you're shrewd about shopping and make the right choices, you'll be capable of purchasing the top high-quality items. For instance, why do you feed your children pre-packaged junk when you can cook the food yourself and be aware of what's inside? Why pay more money for the fact that the factory packed it up and got you to buy it, when you are aware that it's not a good option to feed your family? The food products that come in packages are loaded with preservatives and additives, and there's no reason for you to buy them.

With all the technology available it is possible to make fresh stock pot stew that is packed with plenty of deliciousness by putting the entire ingredients in the slow cooker at night prior to. It is also possible to use fat free cooking using an air-fryer. When you dothis, you'll find that the food you're cooking is healthier, and it will take just a little time. Additionally, there is less cleanup to clean up. After installing an air fryer I've noticed that I don't need to use the oven nearly as much and I don't even have to add too much fat in my diet.

Then, look at the less-important additional items

These are items that you were enticed to buy. Maybe they were put in a specific spot in the store to entice buyers to buy them. The reason behind the design of a shop is carried out by professionals , and they'll nag you each time you allow them to. You must get into the habit of writing an inventory of your purchases and not purchasing anything else. It might sound like it's an exercise however, in the long run you'll bring less clutter into your home, and your house will be more manageable and fun to live in.

Step Five: Shopping for clothes

There is a good chance that your closet is packed with clothes that you don't wear anymore. The reason you are finding it difficult to locate clothes to wear is due to the sheer amount of clothes you must sort through every day to find the perfect outfit. In terms of shopping for clothes is concerned, you'll need to clean out your closet, and this will be covered later in this chapter. But for the moment, you should you should try to reduce your shopping . Tell yourself that unless you believe that the item you're considering purchasing will add value to your life, you shouldn't require it. One of the toughest issues to work about when bombarded by commercials on television and shops that lure shoppers is that they are all possibilities but they're not necessities. There's a possibility that you have a particular collection of shoes however, until you know the exact items you have at home for every occasion, there's no reason to look for another pair to the collection. Be sensible with your approach. You can certainly have an item of footwear when they bring some sort of happiness to your life however, you should consider whether the pleasure will be a novelty that fades out after one time you wear or brings something new to your closet that gives you lasting happiness. It is likely that you purchase items on impulse, so your clothes are filled to overflowing because buying impulse isn't a good idea.

Minimalism doesn't mean sacrificing. It's about having less which implies more. So that gorgeous designer dress you've always wanted is within reach. If you do desire it then what do you have to let go of so that it can find an appropriate spot inside your dresser?

Chapter 7: Home

Have you ever dreamed to return back home at night and see your home clean and tidy and welcoming? It's not always the case that tidy is inviting, so when you tidy one's home the intention isn't to eliminate everything you might need to collect emotions. It's about getting rid of everything that doesn't bring you joy. What number of spare cellphones are you storing away in drawers? How big do you want your television to be? How much furniture will make you feel comfortable, instead of stifling? It is important to move through rooms, and remove items that aren't essential to your satisfaction. If something you own brings you no pleasure allow it to bring another person happiness. It is time to sell it. Remove it and free up space in your house.

The things that can confuse your mind are the mix of colors, the various stimuli that scream to you, and the combinations of colors which make you want to get outside rather than remaining cozy and safe inside your house. There should be at minimum four boxes that you can put items. While you go through your room, make sure you remove the following items:

Things you've not used in the past six months

Medicines that are not up to date

You've tried a few products and are no longer the same

Furniture that makes rooms appear smaller

Colors that are not matched

Things you don't love that you were given by someone else

Clothes you do not wear anymore

Electronics, electronics, and other products you never use more

Let me share with you what's occurred to you. Information overload has you caught in its grip. You've listened to ads. You've been affected by magazines and have become part of the consuming society you dislike. Eliminate it all. It's not necessary to waste money to give the items to charity. Organise a garage sale to make money from the things you have. What you might not be aware of is that the extra space you're opening up in your house can make your life much easier and boosting your efficiency. Let's explain how.

When you clear each area of your home taking your time going through the items within the room and removing unnecessary items, your home will become easier to manage. If you take the time to clean the room after you're done it is possible to introduce new rules for each room. inside the house must be kept cleaner than when you first entered it. Make sure the same rules is applied to all rooms inside your home. You are effectively altering the environment in your home and if your guests want to take advantage of the tranquility it provides and their families, there's an affordable cost to pay to enjoy that privilege. It's nothing to ask for and it can make the lives of children easier by giving them an area they can put their toys. The simpler it is to tidy up for your children easier, the more likely they'll be to obey your rules.

Then, take a take a look at the living area and think about linking the outdoor area to the interior space. It could be done by adding nice furniture for your garden or by letting your yard's landscaping to be visible from your living space. This is also beneficial since it can make your home more comfortable.

Get it done, if you are able to spend more time in relaxation instead of cleaning the mess that is left at home, you can spend more time to spend with the people you cherish. This leads to more rest and that is why when you get to work each day, you're with a sense of revigoration and are able to accomplish more. People who are happier are more productive. If you are able to organize and reduce your home's clutter so that it's all you need instead of everything else that's been thrown in over time and you can take advantage of it more. As we mentioned at the beginning the idea of less always is going always be better. You can see the art work because nothing is getting out of the way. You can see the colors because the walls aren't filled with clutter. You love your kitchen since your work surfaces aren't filled with the appliances that you purchased, but never had the time to start making use of.

I am in love with the simple design of my living space and it helps me simplify my thought process so that I can make plans for the future without anything blocking my thoughts. Additionally I was able to carve an area at home that I can unclutter my thoughts. This is equally important because people who are successful tend to spend time in meditation or listening to music and having the ability to unwind. If you inquire about those such as Richard Branson about work and time balance at home He will be the first to inform you that it's a vital aspect of life, and that he's inspired by the balance is his life. If you're unhappy with your life at home is affecting everything else and the productivity of your employees decreases.

Chapter 8: Allowing You Time To Breathe

It's probably not going to be enough just to clean out your closets and tidy your home and the thoughts that don't have a place at the moment. Also, you must take a moment to relax and breathe. Relaxing in a space which isn't crowded will make it much simpler.

Relaxation exercise

Sleep on your back the bed with the lighting dimmed. If this means you need to pull the drapes, do so. It is likely that if you've gone for the minimalist look that you'll have blinds rather than drapes. They reduce dust and let light to shine into the rooms in your home at the time you require it.

Put your arms to your side. Ensure that you're dressed in comfortable clothes.

Breathe through your nose and hold your breath for a few seconds before letting it go. Breathing should produce an ebb and flow. It's beneficial to place one hand on your abdomen as you attempt to make that rhythm even. Deep breaths and deeper exhales that are a little longer.

Then, close your eyes and visualize the tips of your feet. Move your toes around and feel them tighten. Relax them until they are a bit heavy. This is done for each part of your body starting from your toes upwards to ensure that each area of your body is at ease. Make sure you don't think of other things as you are doing this. Concentrating on just one thing at a given time is beneficial. A little thought can lead to the greatest gains.

While you're doing this exercise, you'll observe the blood pressure drops down, and the heart beat is slowed down. This is why it's crucial to keep this exercise separate from food intake and to allow enough time to get up slowly after having covered all of your body. If you feel it is easy, you can listen to the music you like to relax and there's lots of choices for this kind or music available on Amazon.com as well as various other online stores.

You require some amount of rest for you to move your lifestyle from being materialistic to a minimalist lifestyle. It's a practice that can help you get over the self-doubt that you experience. It is more beneficial to exercising if you maintain it as a regular routine. Relaxation is essential to your mental state and helps you have a good night's sleep.

Don't forget, the fact that you're cutting back doesn't mean you can't take pleasure in great food and an enjoyable lifestyle. Just make changes to your priorities. As an example, wouldn't it be better to prefer to sit down and watch a movie on your TV instead of having the TV on for the entire the time? Make use of the time you would have been sucked up with commercials to do better things.

Take for instance, the book, but be sure to borrow it instead of buying it. You can also make use of a tablet to read the book instead of needing to locate a new place to store the book. The new lifestyle you're living isn't just about having lots of stuff. It's about making the most of the time you're given each day and having a sense of creativity. Reading is a great way to open your mind to new concepts and can be the best option instead of staring at the television screen.

Connect with people that matter to you. You can also pass on the minimalist lifestyle to assist others. But, be aware that you might encounter some resistance from youngsters. If you have young children in your home who prefer the mess in their rooms You can create rules that apply to other areas in the house the rules will be in place. There's no reason to stop you from introducing children to the idea the idea that "less can be more" but you might have to wait until your children are old and have greater knowledge of what consumerism is.

Chapter 9: Rid Of Relationships that are toxic and Nurturing the most meaningful ones using minimal

Most of the time, we form friendships purely out of convenience, without considering the qualities required to create an actual relationship with another person e.g. crucial traits like sharing trust, love for one another and unrelenting support. It is common to keep people around due to the fact that they were already present. A relationship built on the chemistry of a relationship or the proximity between them cannot last.

Consider the connections that you have with colleagues and schoolmates or anyone you've always known around. There are many people who aren't adding anything of worth to your life- without sounding like a snob, or anything. It's possible that you'd rather remain in those relationships since the new ones aren't easy, and existing ones are familiar.

If you feel that someone is draining you, it's the time to take action. You can tell if they're not supportive or hinder your progress and don't contribute value, they just keep taking, without making a difference and continue to play victim. These people prevent you from feeling fulfilled.

But you don't need to live your life like that. A few of the many steps you can consider to address those relationships that are not good for you include:

Take a decision on how to repair the relationship

This is without doubt the most popular option, though it's not always feasible. People change and relationships change, it's life. But, whether it's your relationship, your family or marriage it is possible to change the circumstances without losing sight of the relationship. If you decide to do this the communication will become the most important asset you have.

The first step is to find an appropriate setting (say an espresso shop or diner) and then have serious discussions with the person. Be clear with them about the changes you need to make for your relationship to flourish. Do you need more support? need or do you just want them to be part of your development? Let them know all the details. Be sure to tell them how important they are to you, however in the present, the situation of the relationship isn't making you feel happy. Inform them that you're not looking to change anything about your relationship, you simply want to alter the way your relationship functions. Don't forget to inquire about what they'd like to change. It could be that you're triggering the negative feelings, you never are aware of it. Be attentive and take action accordingly.

Break off from the relationship

It's hard to consider something objectively without bias when you're within the middle of it. If you're involved in a relationship that find toxic and aren't sure if you desire to change the situation or let it go by taking a break, then a break can put you in the right direction. It is also a great option in the event that you've tried to repair it previously but are not seeing any improvement.

Every relationship is naturally complex since humans are that are bound to stumble. If the problems are so severe that they're constantly affecting the way you feel or behave and generally, who you're however you're not sure of the you should do, you should take a break. Let the person you are with know what you think and the reason you're seeking an interruption from your relationship. If you're significant to them, they'll be able to understand.

Think about it write down the pros and pros of the relationship If you must and if it causes more harm than good, you must end the relationship. If you believe there's an opportunity that things might be salvaged, go on to the repair stage.

The end of the relationship

If you've tried but you can't solve the issue, it's time to end it, no matter the person or how difficult it might be. Make it clear and tell the person that you are unable to continue to be with that person and that you must go on. You have a responsibility to be content with having an acquaintance.

Sometimes, leaving is the only way to creating new stronger, more stable and supportive relationships. There are however some exceptions to relationships you're able to quit e.g. an engagement or business partnership, or any other job that can put food on the table. These exceptions may not be applicable to everyone, but when they do it is important to avoid as many of them as is possible. You can also discover a way to get out of them piece by little.

Establishing and maintaining meaningful relationships

For an individual who is minimalist, there's nothing more satisfying than developing connections with others who have similar values and interests. What's the purpose of spending the time with someone who doesn't agree with your values, even though you're getting along well? Therefore, you should seek those who have similar values. It's difficult to grow with someone if both of you are going in opposite direction.

Do your part to maintaining existing relationships. It is also important to bring value to these relationships. It is not necessary to monetize your affection but rather by taking doing things that go out of your way to make sure that the person you love grows, and showing how much you love them. However, it should be a mutual affair And only then can you both be satisfied with your current relationship.

Chapter 10: Principles Of Minimalism

Minimalism is not to be thought of as a philosophy that only focuses on the idea that you have less. It's not a goal in itself , but a method of living that gives you the things you really want. Here are some things minimalist living can bring to your lifestyle.

* It will allow you greater freedom

* It will allow you additional time.

* It will assist you to lessen the stress

It will also increase the pleasure you have

It will assist you to get more efficient with your money.

It can improve your overall health

* It will make room for where the essential things can be placed.

In this sense, Minimalism is governed by the following principles which can serve as a guideline that can guide you to the right path. A few of these principles are:

1. Avoiding unnecessary things. The concept of minimalism can help you avoid unnecessary things that don't bring joy or happiness to your life. This does not mean you should eliminate all things from your life, however, you should only eliminate things that are not beneficial.

2. Finding the most important things. It allows you to recognize those things that are crucial to your overall well-being. These are the things that can make your life more enjoyable and worth it. A minimalist will concentrate on things that can have the most impact on their life and work.

3. Making every moment count. This way of life ensures that you appreciate what you do or do within your daily life. Each action you take taking part in should be considered a part of something.

4. Bring happiness into your life and happiness. The minimalist lifestyle ensures that your life isn't empty , but one that is filled with joy and love for every minute. Your life's purpose should be to contribute worth in the eyes of the whole world.

5. Edit your life. Minimalism is an ongoing procedure that makes sure that you are reviewing your life on a regular basis. It's not an endpoint for itself, but an ongoing review process to help you enhance your life.

Five Dimensions Of Minimalism: Five Dimensions Of Minimalism

The Five Dimensions of Minimalism were created by the writers Joshua Millburn and Ryan Nicodemus in their book "Minimalism Living a Meaningful Life'. The five dimensions are a response of minimalism to the most fundamental notions of happiness for humans that are shaped by consumption and conventional limits. These are the real key areas you should be aware of if you are looking to be happier, as opposed to being content in flashes.

When you are done the chapter, you'll be aware that living a life of meaning depends on these five elements:

* Health

* Relationships

* Passions

* Growth

* Contribution

Now, I will be the details of each of them and how they are related to minimalism.

Health

Wealth is health not just pieces of gold and silver is a well-known, wise saying. This saying is an accurate representation of good health. You can have everything but not be in good health. Wait!!! Does that sound even possible? If we're not in good health our relationships with others could be strained or sour. If we're not in good health the passion we have may be impossible to pursue , and then transform into something worthwhile and productive. If we are not healthy it is impossible to develop ourselves and, without good health we can't be more generous to others as we're unable to give more or even the minimum we can give to ourselves. Health, of course, is the sun that the other four dimensions of happiness and well-being are built.

When we talk of health issues, we don't just talk about being able to prevent death, but also of being healthy and the key to maintaining good health is found in three main things that include eating, playing and sleeping. The first one, eating, doesn't just comprise our meals but also the foods we consume by any means. There is food that we consume that is consumed through the mouth, nose, or even the skin. You must be mindful of what they consume or drink and be sure to stay clear of introducing into one's body anything that can cause harm to the. To do that it is possible to read the most reliable and standard guides to weight loss and adjusting your diet. Follow the rule of "almost all the time, putting into your mouth only what your body requires".

It is a form of exercise, as well as other activities that we can do when we're looking for enjoyment or rejuvenating or revitalizing our bodies. When someone participates in a specific type of sport activity doesn't mean that you have to participate in it as well. Be careful when choosing the kind of sport you'd like to participate in. Pick one that benefits both your physical and mental health rather than one that everyone seems to love.

Sleeping has been shown to bring immense health advantages. Actually, certain people from the oriental world are able to sleep at work due to the fact that they believe that it boosts productivity. Stressed individuals do not improve productivity. It decreases. Sleeping can help the brain reorganize the data it accumulated over the course of awakening. It has also been proved scientifically that you require 8 hours of sleep each night to be healthy.

Relationships

We are who we are surrounded by. The essence of relation to minimalism is that it views the importance of relationships in keeping connections and forming new bonds. As beneficial as relationships are but they are also damaging. How? Negative relationships are common and if they ever do something, it's that they can ruin your life in many ways. If, after reducing the excesses in your life , you have friends who don't honor your decision but attempt to bring you back to the original life of waste Perhaps it's the time to stop engaging in friendship with them. Your relationship with them can be negative because they cause you to feel negative instead of feeling good about yourself.

In the end, your relationships could be classified into one of the 3 categories: required as well as the desired and unnecessary. The necessary are those that which you cannot escape. You can't break the bonds between your parents, your spouse or children. They are the ones that you should be with, no matter if you agree or not. They will not let you go, regardless of what happens unless things drastically change in the worst way. Your boss at work might also fall under this category during certain times of the year. The most desirable are those who your life isn't dependent on , yet their presence within your life with joy, security and satisfaction. Friends fall in this category, if they have quality to your lives. Be aware that those who fall into these first two categories may be in a similar place and those who fall into the second category may require updating to the previous category. The third category consists of the ones that do not add worth to your life and also those that cause damage slowly. In the former case the former, they occupy a small space in your head, and you must eliminate them. The second category is more destructive; they not only take up your time and energy and cause anxiety but also cause your demise and have nothing for your existence. Don't be afraid to cut out these weeds.

Passion

What's life with health and wellness without an area of your life that you are interested in? What will you do during your time? What are you going to do to make a difference in people's lives? How can you channel your passion and energy on self-development? Passion is the key to this. There must be something you can be obsessed with. Do you write? Are you offering community services? Are you involved in a sport? There is no excuse to keep you from taking on your passion. The goal of minimalism is to give you the space to be mentally as well as physical, to be focused on fulfilling your dream.

Growth

He's dead if he does not think about self-development. The person who ignores the growth of his soul, body and self is dead. He is a victim of darkness and is unaware of the cause. He is a burden to humanity, pulling himself back or downwards on an upward slope of growth and satisfaction. This kind of person cannot attain happiness or fulfillment. He's more likely be focused on how to affect the decline of others, and how to hinder the growth of others without realizing it.

The only method of self-growth is when for one to develop in the world. This is the sole thing that gives our lives significance. Living a minimalist lifestyle is one first step towards self-development, but it doesn't stop there. It is essential to continue living not only in search of satisfaction for oneself but also for the lives of others. It is based on this that the next step is connected.

Contribution

This aspect was briefly discussed earlier. It is a result of self-development. It is impossible to claim that we are really growing or advancing in our lives if we can't demonstrate our positive influence in the lives of others or the results that are a result of the result of our own efforts or when working as part of a group. When was the last time that you participated in a community service program that you were able to volunteer for? What did you last did something generosity to the community? Who has helped you in the past? What is the reason to you?

It is important to contribute to the environment, society and humanity, as that is where you will find the peace that we are so eagerly seeking. Therein lays true fulfillment. The sense of satisfaction you feel when looking at a painting or a photo of our home on vacation, or our luxurious vehicle, or the image of us on the cover of the latest fashion magazine cannot be measured against the calm when we remember the ways you have helped others achieve satisfaction.

Chapter 11: Understanding the need for hoarding

Life is filled with amazing memories that are both positive as well as negative. It's only natural to desire to preserve certain memories by keeping a memento or other memorabilia. Tourist attractions and theme parks are filled by gift stores that play on this very same urge to seek out things that help bring back your memories. To a certain extent, it's natural.But as with all problems worrying too much about an item is the time to consider it an problem.

Actually you can be sure that hoarding disorder, which is often referred to as compulsive hoarding, is a real ailment that is recognized by psychiatrists as a mental disorder. It could be anything from holding on to old shoes that don't serve any functional reason, but they have an emotional value, to taking everything you can, including the food wrappers of every product you buy. This disorder was only discovered and classified as an issue in recent times. Before that, people suffering from this condition were usually viewed as pack rats'. No matter where you are in this spectrum of symptoms, you are able to make the difficult , but crucial decision to completely clean your life and concentrate on the future, not take stock of the past.

However, it's an excellent idea to understand the condition you're dealing with. The problem is that psychologists don't completely understand this condition currently. At one point, it was even regarded as an indication of obsessive compulsive disorder (OCD) until it was identified as a distinct disorder. But, even though hoarding disorders that cause compulsive behavior are recognized as a distinct ailment it can be experienced by people who suffer from other illnesses such as OCD or another type of depression, or anxiety. It's good to know that it is only affecting about two-thirds of adults. It usually starts in childhood, and gets more severe as you get older. The good news is that if there is an abundance of things that you've collected throughout the years there is a good chance that you are suffering from obsessive hoarding.

Psychologists can distinguish between collectors and hoarders. While you may see yourself as an avid collector, be aware that you may suffer from obsessive hoarding. Although there is a distinct distinction between the two kinds of individuals, hoarders generally have everything in their possession including chocolate wrappers and car tires and collectors typically keep things that are considered by themselves or by others or others, to be valuable or value, and both, when exercised with the extreme, and can be classified with hoarding disorder.

There is a good chance that if you keep things (or keep the items) then you've likely experienced a trauma throughout your life, particularly during your childhood. This can cause you to keep hold of the smallest of objects. Another reason to consider is that you might be hoarding items in order to fill a sense of emptyness that you feel in the present. You may use the hoarding techniques to fill the void which is caused by not being entirely satisfied with the way you live your life. Maybe you're not happy with your job, maybe you're sad, or maybe you've lost a beloved one, but you haven't found closure over that loss. Whichever the case, it's crucial to embark through a process of self-discovery to find out what could be the reason for your need to hold things that would be useless to most people. A disorder of hoarding can have lasting physical and mental negative effects on your health, so it's essential to address the issue immediately and get to the source of the issue and resolve it earlier instead of later.

Finding the root of the problem may be challenging, but in the end it's the best option to make and you will benefit your mental health overall. If you're having trouble figuring out the reason you are suffering from this condition, take a take a look at your habits of hoarding in general and observe whether you see patterns in the items you're collecting. There could be clues in your collection that speak to you in a way, and can help you determine the root of your problem.

Accept that not addressing the issue won't accomplish any good. It will only result in advancing your situation until it is uncontrollable. So, begin this assessment process as soon as possible and not later than it's too late.

Chapter 12: What's the Best Place Do I Begin?

The process of reducing your clutter can be overwhelming. After all, if you've spent your entire life collecting possessions and things all around, breaking these items to basic necessities can seem like a daunting task.

Many people say they'd like to be able to live with less items, but don't know where to begin. Are you feeling like this?

In addition it's about more than just being able to live with less. It is a way to bring purpose into your life. It helps you clear your head of all mental clutter, take a review your spending habits as well as your lifestyle, and eventually become more aware and better capable of making changes to your life when you need to.

Begin slow. Take one room off one at one period of time. Create a habit of minimalism.

In this chapter, we listed some of the most effective strategies to begin your journey towards minimalist living. It's not necessary to take on all of these in one go Think of this more as an outline for a slow and ebbing path toward a new way of life!

1.) Set Your Goals Straight

First, you have to be interested in the change. I'm sure that when you read this book, that you wish to alter some things in your daily life. It is important to understand what you are looking to accomplish to make the change in your lifestyle a reality. The idea of living with less is incredibly relaxing, but it's nevertheless a significant change and it is easy to slip back to routines in no time. But don't worry - it'll become much more simple to start again every time. Every day, 1% of a change can add up over the long in the long run!

If you're making the change with your family or just as an individual take a look at the main reasons why you wish to change your lifestyle. Some of the reasons include:

You'd like to save some money to eliminate credit

You'd like more space around your home.

You'd like to spend more time with your family and yourself

You're in need of more peace and harmony in your life.

You're looking for experience over things

You do not want to stress about the little things

The reasons you want to live longer can be anything but the most important thing is that you're conscious of you and your family members why you're making these changes.

2.) Develop a Minimalist mindset

A minimalistic mental attitude is more crucial than physically cleaning your home of clutter. It is important to try to get to an area where you don't toss things out simply because no things that and demands you to pay focus. You must enjoy your surroundings.

Being a minimalistic person and a fundamental element of my daily life, is the only way I've stuck with this way of life and know that this for me is the most effective method of living. A minimalist approach to life is all about living your life with consciousness. It is essential to integrate the intention of your actions into your day and be aware of the reasons behind the decisions you make.

3.) Choose a thing to get rid of first

In the end, minimalism is founded on the concept of living with less things. A less cluttered home can help you concentrate on what makes you happy and what you truly require.

However, moving to living a minimalist lifestyle starting by starting from scratch, usually means that some decluttering work needs to be completed first.Choose one space and work on decluttering the area before proceeding to the next. This is the best method to keep from becoming overwhelmed and giving up initially!

Here's a brief list of areas where it's possible to begin:

Your wallet. What was the last time that you utilized all of you "loyalty" credit cards?

Your fridge. Do you have a few months old mayo containers that you previously used but they're now are sitting in the fridge?

- Your computer desktop/phone unlock screen. Don't be overwhelmed by useless icons that need your attention.

Email or mail. They're not designed to be the most efficient task lists. You'll be surprised at how many emails or messages can be dealt with in less than two minutes.

These are very basic examples to get your ball moving. After that, you can move on to more elaborate things A drawer in your kitchen, a closet in your bedroom, one room of the home. Step by step, look for the small items that will get you going.

4.) Stay to a System

A few people begin to declutter and then end having a messier home than the one you started in (guilty!). I tried to get rid of my clothes and then end with piles of unworn clothes I wanted to keep just to be safe'.

To get out of this thinking process is vital!

Here is the steps to declutter your home. Three piles are included:

Keep

Donate

Throw

5) Reduce the TV

TV can encourage us to become lazy, and to be tempted to buy the things that are advertisements in between shows and eventually reduce the creative spark within our minds. If you aren't able to let your TV go but you can at least try to reduce the amount you watch.

Like with shopping - set the timer while watching television. What was the amount of time you watch? If you love watching TV for entertainment, then at the very least, measure how long you spent watching television ads.

6) Plan your Meals

The typical UK households waste PS470 dollars worth of food every year. This is mostly due to a lack of planning. My opinion is that your attitude towards food shopping and cooking on a weekly basis can influence your attitude toward other things within your home.

Chapter 13: Cleaning Out Closets

Congratulations! If you've followed this step-by-step guide you've completed the biggest areas of your house already. There is still a lot of work to complete however, you've accomplished a lot and the rest of it will be completed within a matter of days.

Once you've completed the common areas and bedrooms It's time to take on your closets. In accordance with how big your house there could be many closets. Each one is meant to serve an individual purpose, but often, closets are magnets for diverse items as time passes. It can eventually become difficult to figure out the items that belong in each closet and you find yourself randomly throwing things in where they can be. This chaos can cause frustration and anxiety each time you have to store something in a closet , or discover items you've not been using in a long time. This simple overhaul of your closets will assist to reduce the amount of clutter in each closet. It will also help you organize your belongings so that they're in places that are logical and reduce the stress you feel each time you open the closet door.

Step One Step One Bedroom Closets

Since you've already taken care of your bedrooms, the closets in your bedroom are an obvious extension of the procedure. You'll be proficient sorting out clothes that are no longer needed and other clothes now that you've done the job of transforming the drawers of your dresser. You can now complete the reduction of your clothes in closets.

Complete sorting your clothes. Following the same process that you began with the drawers from Chapter 4, you can now sort through your clothes in your closets in your bedroom. Go back to Chapter 1 for the guidelines of this step of the transformation. Be sure to cut down on the number of similar clothes you own get rid of the emotions associated with clothes sizes that are either too big or too small and get rid of clothes you don't wear anymore or haven't worn ever.

Sort out your shoes and other accessories. If you're female it is likely that you own an excess quantity of shoes. Men aren't the only ones also guilty of hoarding shoes as well. While it might seem as if you require every single pair of shoes you own, that's not the case. The same applies to other accessories like belts, hats and bags, and scarves. Follow the guidelines below to sort these items and you could be surprised by how few you'll have left when you're done

Get rid of any that is extremely damaged. After you've finished you could reward yourself by locating better replacements, unless you realize that you do not require it.

Take out any items you haven't used for the past year.

Get rid of any that do not match an outfit in particular, especially when you don't often or rarely wear the outfit.

Get rid of any you're keeping for sentimental reasons for example, such as wedding decorations from your wedding. If you must keep them, you must find an appropriate method to store them. There's no reason to store them in the same clothing you are currently wearing.

Take off any clothes that appear retro, unless you frequently wear clothing that is retro.

Keep in mind the shoes and accessories that serve many uses, particularly the ones that reflect classic designs. The more events and outfits that they can be worn the more appropriate.

Get rid of things that belong in different areas of your home. If something isn't closely related with clothing items, then it isn't necessary to put it in the bedroom closet. There are exceptions to this rule when you are limited in storage space at home and have to store towels, bedding or office equipment, photo albums, or other items of storage for your household inside your closet. We'll begin getting those things organized in the near future.

It is a good idea to rotate your clothes according to the seasons. If you have storage space within your house such as an attic or basement, it might be beneficial to put off items that aren't seasonal. In winter months, you can keep tank tops, shorts and sandals. In summer, it is possible to store coats and thick winter socks long winter underwear as well as snow boots and sweaters. Vacuum sealed space saver bags are an excellent alternative for compact storage of the things.

Then, organize the rest of the items. For those items that are left attempt to arrange the space as tidy and organized as you can. Hang similar pieces of clothing together. Place shoes neatly together on a rack for shoes or buy an over-the-door hanger if there isn't much space in your closet floor. Belts, purses, and scarves can be hanged by hooks or hangers. If you have some spare cash many department stores have numerous solutions for organizing your closet. Think about buying some of these products to tidy up the way you organize your clothes. You'll be amazed at the relief you feel each time you open the newly-organized closet!

Step Two - Linen Closet

When you've completed the closets in your bedroom, then you're now able to move on towards the laundry room at your house. It is the place the place to store any additional towels and sheets. Many people also store extra bathroom and kitchen items inside their laundry closets. This could include toilet paper and garbage bags, paper towels as well as other items that are normally purchased in large quantities.

Think about reducing the amount of towels and sheets you have. We all have an excessive amount of linens. We appear to be convinced that we cannot ever have enough of these items. Hence, we are inclined to keep old sheets "just in the event" in the event of an emergency.

What kind of sheet-related emergency do we anticipate in the first place?

If you don't have children who are known to regularly wet the bed, you will require no more than two sets of sheets for each bed. This means you only have one sheet set on your mattress, and an additional set that you keep in a closet. That's the only thing you require! In the event that you own a guest room there is a chance that you will have one set of sheets to use for the bed. There's rarely a scenario that you will ever encounter where you are unable to wash sheets in the morning so that it is clean and ready for use in the evening.

In the case of towels, a similar guideline to sheets is to be followed. It is generally accepted that one will not have greater than 2 sets towels for every person within the house. This means that for every person in your home, you will need two hand towels, two washcloths as well as 2 bath towel. It's fine to keep some old towels to be used in the event of pet dries, spills or for other chores that require a lot of effort. In the majority of cases it's not necessary to maintain a fancy "guest sets" consisting of cloths. The majority of guests will be content with your standard towels. Because you likely have two towels for each person you'll have plenty of extra towels for guests.

Reduce and organize other items. While it's perfectly fine to keep extra toilet paper, paper towels and garbage bags neatly tucked away within the closet for linen, there's additional things that can be cut down. If you own a couple of bottles of lotion that were given to you as birthday gifts or Christmas, you might consider giving them back or giving them away. Because you likely use up shampoo conditioner, soap, and shampoo in a relatively short time it is not necessary to store additional bottles of these items also. Buy them as they're empty instead of purchasing large quantities. It is possible to save cost by buying bulk body wash however the peace of head you will get from having uncluttered closets for your linens is worth the additional cents you pay.

Get rid of items that don't belong. See step 3 under "bedroom closets" for details.

Sort out the remaining things. For kitchen or bathroom storage items folded and stacked carefully on shelves. If you're lacking shelves, think about investing in an affordable hanging shelf. If there are a lot of people living in your home who assist with chores such as cleaning up laundry Consider labeling each shelf with things that belong on them. So everyone is capable of adhering to the organization system you've created and won't get overwhelmed by a messy linen closet.

Step Three The Entryway/Coat Cabinet

For the majority of us, the closet that is located in front of the doorway ends up being a storage space for various items. The original intention was that it would be used for storing coats, outerwear, umbrellas and other outdoor gear solely, but over time, we'll end throwing other items out of necessity or just plain lazyness. We throw extra boxes in there, and promise ourselves that we'll take them out of them one day. Children begin to place their books on the floor instead of going to their rooms. And they end up taking place in the closet during summer. Other things are tossed onto the shelf of the closet while we go between home and car. We are always determined to relocate these objects to their proper places at some point however "eventually" doesn't seem to happen. In addition, we tend to keep coats in storage for years after they've been replaced or worn out of utility. What happens from all this accumulation is a closet that's so full with things that you require the crowbar to break apart coats to find the one that is right for you. Now is the time to fix the issue of the overcrowded closet in the entryway. It won't take a lot of time, since you've already learned the process of clearing out and reorganizing the linen closet in the bedroom.

Remove everything. Contrary to the linen and bedroom closets, which may be reorganized in phases The entryway closet is often so chaotic that you have to remove everything in one go. In other words, you might not find a few bags that have been forgotten or shoes in the back corner, or a pile of hats that are a bit dusty on the upper shelf of the closet.

Sort out all the things in the closet. The first step is to divide the things that aren't needed within the wardrobe, like items that need to go to the bedrooms of children or garages. If you find that any of these items don't need to be used then place them in the piles designated to be donated or thrown away.

The next stage of sorting things is to determine what should remain and the things could get rid of. Apply the previous-used rules of clothing for your hats, coats and mittens, boots, umbrellas, and other items that you think is appropriate for the closet in your entryway. Donate or recycle anything you haven't used in the past time period of more than a year, anything that was replaced with the latest model, or something that has a particular purpose that you don't make use of it. For instance, if you own a nice jacket for black tie events consider when was the last time you wore the coat was. You can then decide if there is another coat that would be suitable for wearing over an elegant outfit. Be aware that you must keep things that have numerous uses and eliminate items that have a function that you do not need them. If something is outdated and in poor condition, you shouldn't be holding the item "just in the event" you'll need it even if there is an ideal replacement.

Sort out the rest of the items. It is likely that you have managed to eliminate enough items to be able to locate things quickly and conveniently in the event that you need they from the entryway closet. If you've got a small amount of items to ensure that the dowel floor and top shelf are able to provide enough space to accommodate everything, then there's no reason to purchase any additional storage equipment. If you think that you would be able to benefit from an extra layer of organization, think about purchasing several items that are inexpensive, such as hanging shelves as well as a shoe rack and an overhead hanger which has pockets. Over-the-door hangers are useful for organizing more than shoes. They can be used to store dog leashes, gloves as well as stocking hats for dogs, baggies for poop, and other small objects you would like to grab when you head from the front door. When the pockets are open and visible, you will be able to see through them quickly to find items also.

Step Four - Storage or Utility Closets

Apart from the usual kinds of closets found inside a home, a lot of homes also have closets with extras that we enjoy filling with a plethora of possessions. The things we can store in these storage closets are household maintenance items including cleaning equipment outdoors equipment, storage boxes objects, the seasonal decorations. A closet (or three or two) such as this can be difficult, but once you know the procedure it shouldn't be any trouble.

Determine the function of the closet's purpose. If your house is small in storage space, it's fine to store more than one type of items in a closet. But, you'll need to know exactly what's in the closet to be able to look for items whenever you need they. When you've completed your process of searching your storage closet you will have decreased the number of things in the closet, making this objective is easily achieved.

Sort and remove everything. Like in the closet for coats, get everything out. Find a place for everything that belongs in a different space or room, unless you already discern it as something that needs to be taken away. Then, you can sort all of it into categories such as tools and outdoor equipment, pet equipment household maintenance items storage boxes ornaments, etc.

In each category, you must carefully look over each item and decide whether your life could benefit from keeping it. If you really need it and you use it regularly then keep it. If you are absolutely required to keep it for reasons of nostalgia you should keep it, but think about placing it in a less accessible location in a place like the attic. Closets should only be used for items we must be able to access regularly. If you find that you haven't used something for an extended period of time and you aren't likely to use it for a while, or have duplicates of something that you have, it's probably time to eliminate it.

Then, choose which types of things you'll keep in every closet. Based on the number of closets you have at your home, you might be able to devote one for pet things and outdoor equipment. In another case, you might be able to store items for home maintenance and cleaning. If you need to store everything from each item in the same place you're fine. Do your best to minimize the amount to ensure that everything is arranged comfortably and in a neat and orderly manner.

Reorganize the items that you've tucked away in your closet. Like an entryway, it might be necessary to buy various organizational devices, such as shelves or drawer units made of plastic. It is also possible to label shelves and drawers so that everyone within the family is aware of exactly the place where everything is.

Are there any other closets left?

There may be additional closets that were not addressed in this chapter however, you should know the procedure. When you organize each closet make sure you know the reason for it as well as the categories of items you'd like to store in it. You can then reduce the amount of things by rehoming lost objects and disposing of or donating whenever possible. You might want to consider locating a less accessible storage space for items that you think you need to keep but don't require or need to look at frequently. Then, put the items that you're keeping in the closet in an organized manner. Make use of racks or shelves with a reasonable price when needed Label everything as you'd like!

You'll be amazed by how amazing it is to be able to access clean and clean closets throughout your home. It might have required some time however, your effort will be worthwhile at the end of the day. Being able to locate items and swiftly restore them in their proper location is essential to simplify your life and minimizing the clutter in the clutter in your home.

Chapter 14: The Keys to A Minimalist Lifestyle

This chapter I'll briefly describe what I have learned.

My work is one of the keystones to an uncluttered

life. These are the keys which work to improve

Me, surely for you, it will be other people.

A minimalist lifestyle is easier.

It is more straightforward than it seems. It is more important to keep following

These steps

Buy few but quality:

After the cleaning is completed Keep the firmness and firm

The rule "enter one leave one" so as to not accumulate again. When you purchase fewer items it is possible to

Be more careful about the items you purchase. You

will examine the durability and quality of the product.

of the purchase, and of the purchase, and

sustainable. Make your purchases ethical and sustainable.

Learn to purchase at sales.

Reduce your debts:

Living a minimalist lifestyle means reduction in

your debts, since you consume less,

Only buying what you really need. Having debts

is an ongoing concern in our minds, so keep it in mind.

You can make a plan for reducing your chances of getting them. Your

New purchases are not recommended, so do not purchase anything new.

installments.

Get rid of items that you don't want:

Make a list of your possessions,

Examine each item carefully and identify those aren't

for any reason for you, then sell them.

If they're valuable or are of value, you can either make a donation.

By doing this, you can begin getting rid of things that

There is no need for them at home.

Get healthier:

Limit your intake of food, for example, Late

Benjamin Franklin quote, "To lengthen

Your life will be a lot easier if you eat less." take what you like.

Your body requires and you should stay away from processed food items.

Rest, exercise, drink plenty of water, and

you can begin intermittent fasting, and then

you will discover how your life is going to change and

You feel better when you have sufficient energy

to conquer the day.

Reducing the usage of social media

Many people invest the most beneficial

the time they'll utilize to improve their lives to improve their lives

Facebook, use social media as minimally as you like.

is possible, or it could or it will. Remove harmful

Friends from your list and keep in touch with the ones you like

Positive thoughts. The same is true for positives.

WhatsApp. You can turn off your mobile,

For instance, while I write, I'll turn my

Turn off your mobile to prevent distraction.

Calm your mind:

Be at ease with yourself. Be at peace with yourself.

Present, forget about the past.

If you're gone, you're not there any more.

When you can be outdoors, take a walk in the nature.

Do yoga or meditate to help you find equilibrium

and harmony.

Your well-being doesn't depend on

not having as many things not appreciating what you have

ones you have , and not looking for more

more. The most memorable moments of your life are

Not associated with any object, however, it is associated with an individual or some experience. Think about

That they are simply things!

Finally, those things we keep

"just in the event" can cause us to accumulate and

The accumulation is without any requirements and

functionality. It is important to learn how to appreciate

The real significance of what is important.

Chapter 15: Minimalizing Your Home

"Have none of your houses that you don't know that is useful, or believed to have beauty." -- William Morris

Have a look around your home. What are your thoughts about it? Sure, it's your home, so you are awed by it, but do you actually feel comfortable in it? Do you find it dirty, messy, and not as welcoming as you'd want it to? Do you want your house to be more meaningful to you and share your amazing, beautiful life story? If so, minimalism could aid you in this job.

How to Minimize Your Home's Decor

Here's how to make your home minimalist to make it more unique and memorable to you.

Cleanse Your Home in waves

Don't try to clean your home in one go. This can be very stressful and if you need to dispose of a number of things in one go it can be difficult to think about going minimalist. To make sure you don't abandon your dream of becoming minimalist, start slow and steady. One way to accomplish this is to clean sweep your home in waves.

Use a box to go through the rooms of your house. Spend 10 minutes in each space and put everything that you no longer require or want to use in the box. If you've never ever used a stapler that has been lying around in your study space for a while, put it in the box. If you don't love a certain scarf toss it into the box as well.

After you have completed the first wave, you can go to the next. This time, you should focus on the items that you don't use or do not like. If you own four pairs of jeans , but only wear two then get rid of the two other pairs. If you only use one or two plates, but you have a large number that take up all the space in your kitchen cabinet, clean them out.

After you've completed the second round After that, you can go to the third one and look over your entire home including wardrobes, closets and cabinets. Remove any unnecessary piece of furniture such as cutlery, clothing accessories, makeup dishes, toiletries, utensils books, toys and everything else that's not essential to you any longer. Keep everything that you use regularly and the ones which are meaningful to you. You can share stories about your life. Take for instance the gold medal you received in your first 100-meter race. Also, keep the blue ottoman your grand grandfather gifted you for Christmas. These items add significance to your home and can make it more about the person who owns it.

It is not necessary to complete all three waves in one go. It is possible to spread them out across a period of time as well as weeks. The goal is to make it an enjoyable and meaningful experience that you are inspired to stay minimalist to the end of the tunnel. Therefore you should take as long as you're able to get rid of clutter in your home.

Clean and organize Your House

After you've cleared out your entire house tidy and organize it all. First, dust everything and take care to clean sticky floors or any other items with mop. When your home is clean and span, tidy up everything. Your home will look more inviting and welcoming than ever before.

Create an area that is clutter-free

To feel inspired to live with less than you you'll need, make an uncluttered space within your home. The area should be free of clutter to remind you of your pledge to live a minimalist life and to be content with the smallest and most meaningful items.

The zone that is clutter-free might be your bedroom, your nightstand or an office table, room, or perhaps a cabinet in your living room. Create a space that is always clean and take it as a source of inspiration to transform your entire home into a clutter-free area.

While you make the modifications to your home Keep a journal to write down what you think about them. This will help you keep track of your progress and record how minimal you feel. Review your feelings frequently to see the level of satisfaction you have and also any mistakes you may make.

After you've brought minimalistism to your home, you can apply it to your relationships with family and friends. The next chapter explains how to go about it.

Chapter 16: The Advantages Of Minimalism + How To Implement

The benefits of minimalism to your life will be largely contingent on the kind of life you would like to live and what you cherish.

As minimalism is an effective tool which allows you to build a meaningful, worthwhile lifestyle, one that focuses on the reduction of unnecessary things to ensure that the things you value and significant can be put in the spotlight. The benefits are numerous and as varied as our individual personalities.

The people who have applied the concept of minimalism throughout their life have observed that when you establish the concept as a way of life and then implement it by decluttering and organizing minimalism has these benefits:

It will allow you to experience lasting peace, happiness, and joy and help you live an enjoyable life.

The process of letting go of things that you don't need and whose significance is not in line with what you think is essential or valuable will provide you with the boost you require to get out of debt quicker and save money or have cash on hand to buy things you actually need and bring value to your lives. When you stop letting consumerism rule your life, you will be able to enjoy a more fulfilling life. One in which you are mindful about spending your money and on things that are important and are worth your time, whether it be investing, saving or going on an adventure with your family, or going on a vacation.

Many minimalists who practice have been open regarding the worry free lifestyle of a minimalist lifestyle. In reality the fact that when you have less items to manage or think about--upkeep and protection, etc.-- your stress levels reduce dramatically. As a result of the lower the stress level, you have a feeling of tranquility and ease. Additionally, when your rooms aren't "a bustling hive of activity" it helps reduce visual clutter, which is a well-known factor in stress and anxiety.

This isn't all of the benefits of minimalism. In fact we've only begun to scratch the surface. This page of resources from Becoming Minimalist includes an extensive list of 28 major advantages of minimalism.

This book suggests that you are searching for a way to make minimalism a part of your daily life and declutter your home without feeling overwhelmed. We've got you covered:

The Most Simple Method To Implement Minimalism

Minimalism is about rethinking the significance you place on things and deciding to include only the things that add value and worth in your daily life. You can imagine that creating your life this way is a call for an DELIBERATE decision to make.

It involves decluttering, reviewing and organizing. Decluttering and organization are the key elements of living a minimalist lifestyle. The process of implementing minimalism involves four main steps:

Step 1: Take off

Start with a tiny area such as a corner, space or a single room, take out everything that is in that space. Make sure to reduce the number of steps.

Step 2: Assess

Remove items and other items from any room or space, like the bedroom or TV cabinet in the living room or the kitchen, you should pick each one and assess its significance for you and your daily life.

Marie Kondo, author of four bestseller books about Japanese minimalistism, clearing clutter and organization, advises "As the you take an item in your hands, consider, "Does this spark joy?" "Does it add significance for me?" "Is it valuable?" If an item doesn't answer "yes" to all or any the three questions above, then it has no place in your home or in your environment and is in fact destroying your life's vitality and happiness energy."

If you find things that do not bring joy, or add value in your daily life or don't have any value at all you can place them in a container that is marked for sale or giveaway.

Step 3. Step 3:

After going through your home clearing everything away and assessing its value and significance, arrange the things in different boxes. To get the most efficient cleaning and organizing, you should utilize four boxes - also known as the four-box method, which is labeled (1) retain, (2) storage/not quite sure, (3) trash, and (4) donation or gift.

After holding the object for a few minutes and deciding if it has value, is a source of joy or is meaningful then place it in its appropriate box. Things you're not sure about should be put in the storage or 'not sure' boxes.

The items that are significant, valuable, and that bring joy should be put in the box of keep (the things in this box are those you'll clean, arrange and re-assign to your space that is now clean). For things you do not require, need, or want or are of no value rather than adding to your daily life you may donate, throw away or sell.

Step 4 Clean and restore

Once your belongings have been packed into four boxes take three boxes out of your room (or the space) and begin cleaning and organizing your stuff in the box that you keep, things that make you smile and are significant and important.

This is the real deal. It's all there is to minimalist living and simplifying your life. If you can do this for every aspect of your office space, life-related relationships computers, chores/tasks--you'll make your life easier and turn into a minimalist.

Begin with the the WHY

Every undertaking has a driving drive, a motivation to achieve a certain goal. What is the reason you wish to make your life easier? What are the benefits of minimalism that you hope to extract? Are you seeking to reduce your burden because you're trying to increase your financial stability and relationships, be able to break free from the shackles of consumerism or sell off items that aren't needed to save more money or get that one thing you're looking for to live a blissful life? Write down the things that are driving you to reduce your clutter or live an easier, more meaningful life.

Particularly write down the lifestyle and experiences you wish to enjoy once you clear and organize your home and spaces. You can then relate it to how minimalist living will assist you in reaching your goals.

The more closely you connect in yourWHYs or your motives to begin a minimalist and decluttering journey The more enthusiastic you will be which will increase the likelihood to stay committed to your goal--the 30-day decluttering and organizing challenge.

The remainder of this book offers a step-by-step method for simplifying your life by organizing, decluttering as well as simplifying life in a relaxed way within 30 days.

Chapter 17: Cleaning Your Space

"One can decorate a room with a lavish style by taking out furniture, rather than placing it back in." -- Francis Jourdain. 1876.

Unorganized spaces can lead to unorganized thoughts, a lack of focus and general lack of discipline in our lives. If there's clutter around us, we are likely to lose motivation and become unproductive. It is important to get rid of the negative energy that is associated with disordered environment. Decluttering is believed to be beneficial for those who are practicing it.

The Step by Step Guide to Decluttering

After we have a better understanding of the consequences of living in an unorganized space, let's start to purge.

The first thing you should do is figure out where to place documents and papers. Paper is the main source of the clutter that is in the home. Select a box or container that can be able to hold your documents while you gather them. This will make it easier to sort them later on and ensures there isn't any lost in the route.

Begin with a small. Select a small area of an area and begin cleaning it. Don't place anything in the area in the event that it is not needed or is utilized. Keep working until the entire home is completely fully covered.

Choose the right surface. It can be a shelf or countertops. Take out the unnecessary and keep only the things that are important to the surface, such as flowers or a book you have read many times.

Schedule time for decluttering. The majority of the time , people are busy at work or school and don't have the time to be at home to take care of the house. Choose a weekend or a time when you can take a break and clean your home. Invite your family and friends to be also involved. This can make the process more enjoyable and assist in making progress even in the event that you fail to complete the task by the close of the break. You can finish the work by yourself.

Locating places to store things you frequently use can be a huge help. These are the things you always look for, but you never ever have a suitable space to place them. Explore the home and you will be able to find places where you can place them. When you locate places to put other things around the house You will see the home begin to tidy up, and finding places for items you don't need will be easier.

The cables in your home are increasing. Every home nowadays is equipped with multiple electronic devices that have cables. In time, these cables build up and can be a nuisance to look at and separating them is difficult. You can separate the wires in the same device, and then tie them using Zip-ties, or even black tape.

Before beginning the process of decluttering first, take a step back and imagine where you would prefer everything to be when you're done with the process. This will give you a direction and can cut down on the time wasted trying to determine which areas to put everything. It also aids in getting rid of items that do not belong, and free more space.

Sometimes , you're not sure about whether to keep or give away. Set these items aside for a period of time. Put them on your calendars, so that you can remember to keep track of it. Most of the time, there's not much of importance but if you find something, you should remove it. The rest can be put out.

Decluttering is a great chance to give away. The process of cleaning your house reveals clothes you did not use and those which no longer fit alongside other things such as toys and other dishes. Giving them away to the less fortunate helps us to play our part to improve the lives of those who are less fortunate than us.

Create a list of items to consider before you purchase. This is not necessary for items like clothes, electronics and accessories. Keep the list for approximately a month. If you are still tempted to purchase something on the list, buy it. In most cases, you will notice that the need to purchase the items will disappear within a month. This technique helps in limiting the accumulation of useless items and also saves money by cutting down on impulse shopping.

Train yourself, your kids roommates, significant others and other family members the importance of cleaning up and tidying up after themselves. This helps reduce how much clutter builds up in time. Maintain this routine until you're comfortable with it.

When you get home with something new, you should take something else in the place. It is usually the item you're replacing with, but it may also be that's similar in size or greater. This reduces clutter.

Create a folder or file to organize your documents to ensure that they don't hinder your work. Also, keep extras for the event that you need to establish a new category.

Each time you have to organize paperwork, decide how you can deal with them in a timely manner. Place them in the appropriate file or dispose of them in the event that they're of no value. If you're unable to determine what you should do on the moment, take a note and put the documents in a folder for future actions. Don't put them back in the pile from which they came; it could undo all your efforts.

If you notice something that you do not use when you go about your home, you can put it in a bin and either throw it away or donate it. This can be done for clothing or notebooks, accessories, as well as kitchen equipment. This can help you declutter your house gradually until everything serves a purpose.

Take a look at the medicine cabinet as well as drawers. Many of the items within these spaces are not being used or ignored. Start by taking everything out and sorting them into piles. Everything you require goes to the drawers and cabinet. Products that are not used or in use are tossed out, while items that are not used get donated to.

Take pleasure in the results of your hard work. Enjoy how nice everything appears when it's all organized. Keep your home neat and tidy and you'll see an improvement in your overall outlook, such as improved confidence and overall efficiency.

Change Your Decor and Aesthetics an edgy look

To make the most of your newly cleared space, changing to a minimalist look to your living space is a great idea. Simple decor will help you maintain your home's order since there's not much to do in the house. The look might seem easy enough to accomplish however, it can turn out to be difficult to achieve.

First step coming up with a color base. It is recommended to choose the most laid-back hue, which is usually connected to white. This is due to the fact that it induces peace and tranquility. However, this doesn't mean it should look boring. You can inject a bit of colour, but be sure it is able to blend in with earthy tones and Tans. It's then a matter of what you should put on the wall. With a neutral foundation the decision of what to put in it can be more difficult than it seems. All seems to be suitable. You should pick items that everybody will love. Choose items that are of high quality. If you are limited in the amount of things you can include in your space Make it the best. The environment will be grateful.

The space that is left open by this design gives you the opportunity to experiment and create focal points. Clearing the surfaces gives you the chance to alter the content you show in the small space. Make sure to stick with simple items. Place two or three photos within the space, and then add the vase with flowers. Don't go overboard.

If you think the room could be more vibrant, select an object that is striking and place it on the wall. This could be something that is distinctive, depending on what you like. It can help break the ice when you're hosting guests.

To make your space more exciting, include textures with similar hues. It is also possible to select items of the same color , but in different shades. The addition of a pattern can create a more exciting experience. Introduce colors that naturally blend.

Select a sleek, simple storage solution. It will add to the modern look while keeping your clutter from view. You can always repurpose the old furniture to bring it into with the design of your home, and apply it in the same manner.

Make use of natural light. Do your best to not block the light coming into your home. Make use of sheer or thin curtains or blinds to provide privacy, but leave windows open if you are able to.

Make sure you use clean lines and smooth edges. To keep with the theme of simplicity, be sure your light fixtures, accessories and cabinet handles are simple design. The flat surfaces are ideal as well as left unobstructed.

The switch to minimalist décor helps keep the house tidy by removing unnecessary items in the home. It doesn't need to be just a pile of trash in the room. If there is lots happening in our space in terms of decor, it could interfere with the flow of aesthetics and overwhelm the senses.

Can Minimalism be integrated in Family Time?

Minimalism is growing in popularity and is becoming an increasingly accepted way of living. It emphasizes that smaller is better. The less you need to take on you have more space and time you can use to focus on other aspects in your daily life. Although minimalism is an individual choice in lifestyle parents and caregivers are able to incorporate it into their family and enrich their lives in the process.

There are many reasons that minimalistism should be an integral part of families. The psychological and health benefits of living an uncluttered lifestyle are numerous. It's generally more comfortable to live as the minimalist lifestyle, in addition to other reasons. It's important to remember that making the switch to a minimalist lifestyle as a family may be difficult because we are having to deal with different people with different needs.

If you are a minimalist, you may want your family members to share in the liberating experience, but you aren't sure which way to go about it. Begin by removing your belongings and not compel anyone else to eliminate.

The path to becoming a minimalist household should start by assessing what is important to us as families and deciding on which items to eliminate and what you want to keep. It's a good idea to start as an experiment, and move on as you go. Kids like to participate in family activities , without needing to be taught how their lives are set to alter. Get rid of distractions in your life so that you can concentrate on making your life more enjoyable. Be sure to not overlook their needs as a result of this shift. You can show your typical levels of love and affection, then others may convince them to join in your cause. Beware of judging others for what they does and don't press them to make a change immediately It will cause them to feel frustrated and untruthful. Don't leave them from knowing the work you're doing. Make sure to explain the process you are doing and inform them about the benefits. Include examples for the children to help them comprehend. Let them know that what you're doing will benefit others with a need, and encourage them to feel empathy. In the end, don't do this on your own and risk believing that you're in the process of going through the motions. It is possible to give them reasons to resist the subject of change. They will figure it out instead of you telling them what they should do.

To begin the process begin by making note of all your belongings and everyday routines. Get rid of anything that is useless or wastes your time. Keep the things that are special and makes your family more close like family gatherings or games. Create a list or board and display it to encourage the rest of the family to stick to the plan. The process of removing time and space wasters can be extremely rewarding. The time you would otherwise spend watching TV or playing video games frees up time to do something else more important. Giving away toys and clothing that are no longer needed makes space and clears the house. These three areas don't require a lot of search or emotional investment, and are , therefore, the easiest to eliminate on the priority list. Don't even think about organizing. The purpose of the change isn't to arrange, but to get rid of the unnecessary activities in your life and free the time to pursue other pursuits. Plan these activities in advance in order to avoid them being lost. Stop expenditures if they are not for food or other necessities.

The children should be involved. Getting children involved in the process ensures that they are learning quickly and progress into a more gradual transition. Begin by creating an example. Your children should be able to see that you are doing exactly what you want them to perform. Also, make sure to give specific instructions to ensure they are aware of what to do. Set up the habit of giving in your child by encouraging them donate things they don't need or require. Establish a place to donate items around the house. Let the children categorize their belongings into categories, so they can interact with each item to determine if it's something they would like to keep it. Set limits for their belongings, to ensure they don't pile up things they don't really need. If they are sharing a space make sure they have designated zones in which they can showcase their belongings. If they run out of space the room is rearranged to remove items that they do not need.

Minimalism doesn't have to be about the elimination of the physical items. However, it does assist in becoming thankful and grateful of the things we own. It also makes the vision of the family more clear and parents can take decisions with confidence that impact the entire family.

There is plenty of free time to be utilized to bond with family members and travel. Activities that families take part in as a unit strengthens the bonds of the family. Making this transition together as a family can be enjoyable, and for kids, they are able to carry these lessons to adulthood. With perseverance and determination it is definitely possible to come up with a plan that is a success for all.

Make more storage available for them, fights about space, conflicts with barred areas of the house being used for storage by the hoarder and loss in confidence if the family tries to tidy these spaces.

Children are at risk of having poor development and social lives because of health issues that are more likely to be triggered by the filthy house and the shame they will be feeling after inviting friends over only to be discovered to live in filth. Parents might also restrict their children from inviting guests to join them due to their shame. The kids may feel anger towards the person whose lifestyle causes their sporadic social interactions. They could also be dissatisfied with the choice they make during a dispute, whether it's the one who has a lot of stuff and the other who doesn't. If a neighbor becomes aware of the issue and becomes concerned, they might decide to report the situation to the authorities and children could be removed to their parent on reasons of child endangerment.

Conclusion

.Thanks for getting to the conclusion in this text. We hope that it was helpful and will provide you with the tools you need to meet your goals no matter what they might be.

This book is a sincere attempt to clarify the benefits of minimalism as well as the ways to implement the idea of minimalism into your household.

This book tries to offer a variety of methods to include everyone in your family, including children.

It also provides options to take action with the idea , even when some members of your family don't support it at this point.

With strategies for decluttering every room of your home to specific methods to help you eliminate items in your house, this book has attempted to cover all aspects of the subject.

I'm sure it has succeeded in bringing awareness to the idea and you'll be able to reap the advantages of minimalism.

www.ingramcontent.com/pod-product-compliance
Lightning Source LLC
Chambersburg PA
CBHW071838080526
44589CB00012B/1042